MW01139679

DRIVERLESS CARS

Ryan James

A Stingray Book

SEAHORSE
PUBLISHING

Teaching Tips for Caregivers and Teachers:

This Hi-Lo book features high-interest subject matter that will appeal to all readers in intermediate and middle school grades. It may be enjoyed by students reading at or above grade level as well as by those who are looking for age-appropriate themes matched with a less challenging reading level. Hi-Lo books are ideal for ELL readers, too.

Each book appeals to a striving reader's age and maturity level. Opportunities are provided for students to read words they already know while encountering a limited number of new, high-interest vocabulary words. With these supports in place, students will read more fluently while increasing reading comprehension. Use the following suggestions to help students grow as readers.

- Encourage the student to read independently at home.
- Encourage the student to practice reading aloud.
- Encourage activities that require reading.
- Establish a regular reading time.
- Have the student write questions about what they read.

Teaching Tips for Teachers:

Before Reading

- Ask, "What do I know about this topic?"
- Ask, "What do I want to learn about this topic?"

During Reading

- Ask, "What is the author trying to teach me?"
- Ask, "How is this like something I already know?"

After Reading

- Discuss how the text features (headings, index, etc.) help with understanding the topic.
- Ask, "What interesting or fun fact did you learn?"

TABLE OF CONTENTS

WHAT IS A DRIVERLESS CAR?

A driverless car is a car that drives by itself. It needs little or no help from a human driver.

It uses **sensors** to read the environment.

It is able to navigate a route without help.

THE FIRST DRIVERLESS CAR

The first driverless car was created in 1925.

Inventor Francis Houdina demonstrated a car that was controlled through a radio.

The radio gave instructions to shift gears, honk the horn, and turn on the engine.

FUN FACTS

NASA (National Aeronautics and Space Administration) has used driverless technology to control rovers on Mars.

SHOWING THE WORLD

At the 1939 World's Fair, General Motors introduced their driverless car.

It used an **electromagnetic** field and metal spikes in the roadway to drive.

Just like Francis Houdina's model, it was radio-controlled.

NAVLAB 5

In 1995, Carnegie Mellon University researchers tested their driverless car, NavLab 5, from Pittsburgh, Pennsylvania, to San Diego, California.

The journey took 2,797 miles (4,501 kilometers) and was successful.

NavLab 5

The only things the researchers had to manage were the braking and speed control.

FUN FACTS

The NavLab 5 was a 1990 Pontiac Trans Sport.

COMPUTER VISION

Driverless cars have specific parts that help them drive.

One part is the computer built into the car. It receives information that helps it control the car.

The computer's information comes from sensors that are placed all around the car.

The computer and sensors work together to create a system known as computer vision. Computer vision is how the car knows its surroundings and its environment.

SENSOR FUSION

Inputs from many sensors are combined, or fused.

Sensor fusion creates a network of information that lets the car's computer vision detect nearby cars, traffic speed, and lane markings. This is similar to how people see the road.

Data from the sensors helps the car's computer know how to react and when to stop.

FUN FACTS

An electric bus with no driver hit the roads in Finland in 2016.

GPS IN CHARGE

Driverless cars have location ability.

They use a **GPS** to know where to go and where the passenger's destination is.

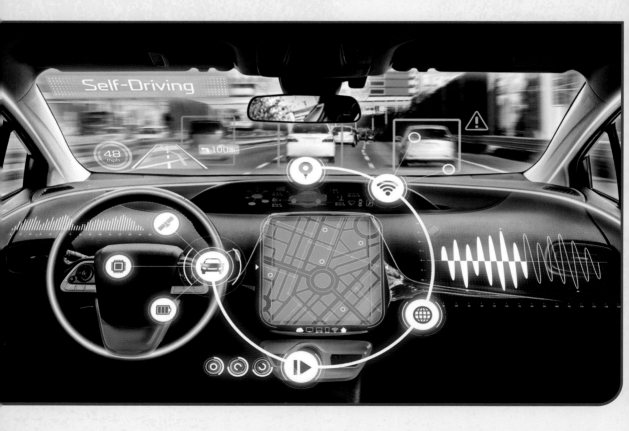

A GPS uses satellites in space to locate specific positions on the surface of Earth.

Driverless cars also rely on **radar** to avoid hitting trees, bike riders, and obstacles in the road.

LEVELS ONE AND TWO

Driverless cars have five levels.

At level one, help from the driver is still needed.

Lane assistance and **cruise control** are part of this level. These features are available on many cars.

Level two has more **automation**.

The car's computer can change the speed and steer on its own.

Vehicles from Tesla, Volvo, Audi, and other carmakers have these features.

LEVELS THREE, FOUR, AND FIVE

At level three, the car can drive itself. But conditions must be **ideal**.

The Audi A8 is one car that has these capabilities.

At level four, the car can self-drive on most roads and in most conditions.

Waymo, a Google company, is testing level four vehicles.

A level five car drives all on its own. The driver may or may not have the option to control it.

GLOSSARY

automation (aw-tuh-MAY-shuhn): the use of machines rather than people to do jobs

cruise control (krooz kuhn-TROHL): a system that automatically controls the speed of a vehicle

electromagnetic (i-lek-troh-mag-NET-ik): of or relating to magnetism that is created by a current of electricity

GPS: acronym for global positioning system; a system that uses satellites in orbit around Earth to help users locate objects and navigate vehicles

ideal (eye-DEE-uhl): perfect, best, or most suitable

lane assistance (lane uh-SIS-tuhns): a system that automatically keeps a car in its lane or that alerts a driver when a car begins to drift out of its lane

radar (RAY-dahr): a way to find things by reflecting radio waves off them and receiving the reflected waves; *radar* is an abbreviation for radio detection and ranging

sensors (SEN-surz): devices that detect and measure changes in the environment and transmit the information to a computer

INDEX

AFTER READING QUESTIONS

1. When was the first driverless car created?

2. What was NavLab 5?

3. What is sensor fusion and how does it help driverless cars?

4. What can a driverless car do at level 3?

5. What do you think are some advantages and disadvantages of driverless cars?

ABOUT THE AUTHOR

Ryan James lives in Western North Carolina with his dog Bailey. His favorite race to watch is the Daytona 500. His dream is to own a Lamborghini. When he's not writing books, you can find him backpacking through Pisgah Forest, North Carolina.

Written by: Ryan James
Design by: Kathy Walsh
Editor: Kim Thompson

Library of Congress PCN Data
Driverless Cars / Ryan James
Car Mania
ISBN 978-1-63897-475-8 (hard cover)
ISBN 978-1-63897-590-8 (paperback)
ISBN 978-1-63897-705-6 (EPUB)
ISBN 978-1-63897-820-6 (eBook)
Library of Congress Control Number: 2022933181

Printed in the United States of America.

Photographs/Shutterstock: Cover & Title Pg © haireena, ©VoodooDot, ©Urse Major, ©4045; Pg 3, 6, 8, 10, 12, 14, 16, 20, 22 ©Urse Major; Pg 7, 11, 14 ©Mooam; Pg 4 ©Gorodenkoff; Pg 6 ©Library of Congress; Pg 7 ©BEST-BACKGROUNDS; Pg 8 ©@Wiki; Pg 9 ©Volodymyr Krasyuk; Pg 10, 11 ©@Wiki; Pg 12 ©metamorworks; Pg 13 ©Zapp2Photo; Pg 15 ©SariMe; Pg 16 ©metamorworks; Pg 17 © AlexanderTrou; Pg 18, 20 ©Audi Website; Pg 21 ©Sundry Photography

Seahorse Publishing Company

www.seahorsepub.com

Published in the United States
Seahorse Publishing
PO Box 771325
Coral Springs, FL 33077